# Burnout & Compassion Fatigue:

## A Guide For Mental Health Professionals and Care Givers

Christine Florio,
MSW, LPC, LADC

# Preface

The concepts and ideas in this book are not intended as a replacement for effective supervision or treatment with a credentialed mental health professional. It is strongly recommended that if you, or anyone you know, suffer from any of the outlined forms of burnout or compassion-related stress, consultation or treatment with a professional therapist should be sought.

Although the title is geared toward mental health clinicians, many other professionals in other disciplines, such as doctors, nurses, police officers, administrative staff, or anyone else that provides face-to-face services for people in crisis may benefit from reading this book.

It is my sincere hope that the information contained in these pages can bring to light many of the challenges faced by mental health and other professionals, validate some of their own experiences, and serve as a guide for prevention.

# Acknowledgments

I would like to first thank my daughter, Kaitlyn, to whom I dedicate this book. She is the light of my life, whose unending love, patience, and understanding of my career far surpasses any gift that I have received in this life. She is, and will always be, my baby girl.

I also want to thank my parents, David and Kathryn, whose support, encouragement, and love has gotten me through some very difficult times in my life. They have made the best times of my life even more worthwhile.

Thank you to my sister, Amy, who always knew I would do this, even before I did. Her strength, courage, and resilience are true inspirations to me.

I need to thank my husband, John, for his support, and hard work that have made it possible for me to keep my head buried in my computer and not in a laundry basket. He has been my rock.

I would also like to thank and give praise to my mentors, Sam Segal and Alan Nolan, at Connecticut Counseling Centers, Inc., who somehow managed to help me believe in myself as a professional, especially during times when no one else seemed to. Their guidance, supervision, and expertise have kept me looking forward more than once, and inspired me to write this book.

I would like to thank the talented and gifted staff at Connecticut Counseling Centers, Inc., whose outstanding work and support for one another has made what we do so much more special and wonderful.

Thank you to Daniel Twaddle; Eric Hahn, R.N.; and Officers Scott P. McCue, Frank Koshes, and Mike Papelo for their input, help and insight from the "front lines."

And finally, I need to acknowledge Robert A., who taught me the valuable lesson that through adversity come strength, courage, and success, and that despite the obstacles, failure was *never* an option.

*Christine Florio*

# Table of Contents

# Introduction

The challenges that face the mental health field are unique, complicated, and sometimes very stressful. The demands placed on professionals to stay "on top of their game" through continued education, licensure, specializations, and trainings can almost be considered another full-time job. Meeting these expectations, as well as the actual provision of clinical counseling, required documentation, referrals, billing, bookkeeping, and various other tasks involved in the process, can lead to a stressful environment.

With the health care industry in a state of upheaval and the restrictive oversight of managed care companies, mental health professionals have had to "learn as they go" as to how to navigate a very complicated system. In addition, the incidents that occurred on September 11, 2001, and more recently, the earthquakes, hurricanes, flooding, and oil spills, have led us to focus our attention on training counselors to provide highly specialized crisis and trauma-related services. Counselors treat not only the families and survivors of terrorism and natural disasters, but also emergency medical personnel, firefighters, police officers, and witnesses. Military personnel and families require their own specialized treatments as well, as veterans returning from overseas often face war-related symptoms of post-traumatic stress disorder (PTSD), anxiety disorders, depression, and substance abuse disorders.

The complications of organization and administrative duties together with treatment and assistance for traumatizing and devastating national events place even more challenges on today's mental health professional. The risks of burnout, fatigue, and vicarious trauma have risen a great deal, leading the profession to give even more attention to PTSD as a problem not only for victims, but for caregivers as well. As mental health professionals are committed to the practice of empathy in treatment, such powerful influences can result in symptoms that are similar to, or the same as, those experienced by their clients.

This book will outline the different types of compassion stress that a practitioner can face at any point in his or her career, from student to seasoned, licensed professional. It is a form of self-treatment so that he or she can lead a long, satisfying career while helping to develop and

Although burnout is a common phenomenon, it has the potential to become an issue of greater impact. Our society has faced great challenges in recent years, and critical incidents such as terrorist attacks and natural disasters have raised the bar for issues of clinician self-care. Although there has been a recent increase in discussion on the topic, very little definitive research has been done to highlight compassion fatigue as a major concern. Despite the availability of resources, these resources are usually limited to burnout and compassion fatigue once it has risen to the level that affects job performance and personal functioning. There is little available to address the telltale signs of burnout and compassion fatigue as they begin to surface.

The key to proper self-care of the clinician and the preservation of a solid clinical relationship is prevention. It is crucial to recognize and address signs and symptoms early when it can be much more cost effective for the clinician, the client, and organizations as a whole. So, why then, do we wait to address these issues later, rather than sooner?

This book serves a tool for a clinicians, caregivers, and supervisors to help identify, understand, and recognize burnout and compassion fatigue, and to provide simple and effective methods for intervention.

# BURNOUT AND COMPASSION FATIGUE

A Guide for Mental Health Professionals and Caregivers

Christine Florio, MSW, LPC, LADC

"We helpers are professional commiserators. We share in life's sadness and stressors; we must understand when no one else might; metaphorically, at least, we stand between our clients and the cruelties they face daily...The price is worth it, of course. Most of us love our job and our life work. But perhaps some perspective offered here may insure that the price is not so high." [1]

"Helping professionals who listen to the stories of fear, pain, and suffering of others may feel similar fear, pain, and suffering because they care. Helping professionals in all therapeutic settings are especially vulnerable to 'compassion fatigue' and include emergency care workers, counselors, teachers, school administrators, mental health professionals, medical professionals, clergy, advocate volunteers, and human service workers. The concept of compassion fatigue emerged only in the last several years in the professional literature. It represents the cost of caring both about, and for traumatized people." [2]

1   Copyright © Dr. Charles Figley. *The Art and Science of Caring for Others without Forgetting Self-Care*, (2007)

2   Copyright ©Rosemary Thompson, *Compassion Fatigue: The Professional Liability for Caring Too Much*, (2003).

# Chapter One:

# What Is Burnout?

Burnout, empathic failure, compassion stress, and compassion fatigue are just a few of the terms used when referring to the emotional dynamics that can occur with counseling professionals at any time. Caregivers who are chronically faced with the painful emotional challenges of their clients have limited systemic resources, experience acute traumatic events and chronic workplace stress are all directly and indirectly at risk of compassion fatigue. Burnout and compassion fatigue in mental health professionals, if not recognized or treated, is the result of listening and tending to the emotional problems and crises of clients on a daily basis. It is the removal of the ability to detach effectively and emotionally from the client's experience, creating a vicarious state of crisis or trauma in the clinician.

This form of chronic stress reaction is also the result of the failure or inability of the clinician to effectively apply and utilize self-care techniques inside and outside of the counseling session, so that they may remain emotionally and spiritually sound and provide effective services to their clients.

The *Merriam-Webster Collegiate Dictionary* defines burnout as the "exhaustion of physical or emotional strength or motivation, usually as a result of prolonged stress or frustration." It is something that gradually builds to a breaking point, and the stress and frustration come from all types of work-related sources.

The most common progression of stages includes the following phases:

- Burnout
- Compassion fatigue
- Emotional exhaustion

These phases do not always occur in linear fashion, and can be dependent upon many factors, such as

- occupational setting;
- availability of professional supervision;
- predisposition to, or comorbidity of mental health problems;
- client population;
- availability of peer support;
- work history; and
- personal, non-work-related stressors

Burnout happens in phases and leads to such problems as impaired decision making, ethical conflicts, and other problems that affect the patient-to-counselor clinical process. Any form of emotional overload that is affecting the ability to function or perform on the clinical or personal level places a counselor at risk for many types of emotional, physical, or occupational distress. Although burnout does not happen to everyone, it is important to learn what it is, how to recognize it, and to intervene early. The earlier that intervention takes place in the form of self-care, the better the prognosis is for avoiding such syndromes such as compassion fatigue and secondary traumatic stress disorder.

The following illustrates the stages of burnout: (Weiss 2004).[3]

**Enthusiasm**–This is the stage early in a counselor's career, or early after changing jobs or roles, where the counselor is

---

3  Weiss, L. (2004) Therapist's Guide to Self-Care. New York, NY

motivated, enthusiastic, and gives 110 percent to his or her job. This is the stage where a counselor feels compelled to prove his or her mettle as a professional and try to make known his or her place in the community. During this stage, it is common to bring work home, work overtime, weekends, or through vacations in order to establish a footing in the workplace. Ideals guide clinicians through their work, as they constantly strive for excellence and a perfect world. Expectations are high, idealistic and somewhat naïve. Clinicians often can be over-zealous, uncomfortable with boundaries, and may let sessions run over time limits in an effort to make an "extra effort." They will take on extra projects or unassigned tasks, in an effort to put their "best foot forward." At this stage it is most effective to "rein in" the overzealousness and replace it with expectations that are more realistic to avoid burnout and compassion stress.

**Stagnation**–In this stage, the clinician feels "in a rut", caught in the middle of a routine, lacking in variety, or feels little challenge. The enthusiasm for work has subsided, and more emphasis is placed on personal, financial, and career/promotional matters, little joy is found in work, and there is little or no motivation to make any extra effort beyond what is expected. At this stage, the best remedy is to provide variables to make the work less mundane; taking a course, joining organizations, utilizing supervision, and developing a fuller personal life can help this stage from progressing.

**Frustration**–This is the stage in which clinicians develop feelings of hopelessness and/or powerlessness. They begin to question the effectiveness of therapy with difficult or unresponsive clients, feel relief when clients cancel, and question the profession in general. At this stage that emotional, physical, or behavior problems can develop. Clinicians may become demanding, pushy, or even verbally abusive toward their clients. They may depersonalize the people they are working with by referring to them as a diagnosis (e.g., "the bipolar" or "the borderline"). Unhappiness and discontent are prevalent. Action is necessary to regain contentment and satisfaction as a helping professional. This might involve evaluating the stage and level of change that is required; changing positions, work hours, or agencies; or, in some cases, leaving the field altogether.

**Apathy**–This is last stage of discontentment listed by Weiss, and the most severe. At this point, high levels of frustration lead the clinician into a state of mind where he or she functions on "automatic pilot," often giving standard responses and interventions in sessions, collecting a paycheck, and going home. Apathy is a form of self-protection to get through the days and years until retirement. This is the most dangerous of stages, as the clients who have trusted the apathetic clinician with their well-being often suffer consequences. Remaining active in home and community life can reverse apathy by providing other means of satisfaction to the clinician who feels overwhelmed. Finding new activities, hobbies, or interests outside of the home can help reverse apathy to a new motivation for career involvement. Active self-care techniques, mental health treatment, clinical supervision, and peer support are other methods of avoiding or decreasing the symptoms at this stage.

Pines, Aronson, and Kafry define burnout as the "state of physical, emotional, and mental exhaustion caused by long-term involvement in emotionally demanding situations" (1988)[4]. This progressive form of stress reaction can result in feelings of emotional exhaustion, depersonalization, and the reduction in feelings of personal and professional accomplishment (Perry 2003)[5]. Burnout is a gradual process, and if not recognized and addressed in its early stages, it will become progressively worse and more difficult to treat. As the negative emotions increase, the tendency to suppress them also increases, leading to general apathy, reduced productivity, preoccupation, and

---

4   Pines, Aronson, and Kafry (1988). Career burnout: Causes and cures. New York: Free Press

5   The Cost of Caring: Child Trauma Academy--Bruce Perry
*http://childtrauma.org*

resistance. These emotions and behaviors are then projected onto the clients and eventually, the organization or system as a whole, creating an environment for further progression of compassion fatigue.

Burnout is more than feeling frustrated or tired. In the progressive stages of burnout, clinicians can feel so depleted that the idea of taking on additional duties seems impossible. The emotional exhaustion or numbness that results from burnout can lead to feelings of resentment toward clients, avoidance of them, detachment from other people, and preoccupations about leaving the career altogether. The symptoms mimic the symptoms of a depressive episode; however, these feelings are not due to loss or grief, but from excessive stress, being overwhelmed, and fatigue. If burnout is not addressed, and evolves into compassion fatigue or exhaustion, a major depressive episode may result. (Weiss 2004) [6].

6  Weiss, L. (2004) Therapist's Guide to Self-Care. New York , NY : Brunner-Routledge

# Chapter Two:

# What is Compassion Fatigue?

Compassion fatigue is, on the surface, the failure to provide a client with the empathy required in a productive counseling relationship. However, this process is much more complex than that. *Also referred to as "compassion stress," "secondary trauma," or "vicarious trauma," this level of stress often* occurs when clinicians closely identify with the client through countertransference and personally absorb the patient's trauma or pain. Compassion stress is a response to the *people* who are suffering rather than to the *work* situation. It does not result from being busy, but from giving high levels of energy and compassion over a prolonged period to those who are suffering, often without experiencing the positive outcomes of seeing patients get better. (McHolm 2006). [7]

Compassion fatigue is not pathological in the sense of mental illness, but is considered a natural behavioral and emotional response that results from helping or desiring to help another person suffering trauma or pain.

There is a great deal of confusion with regard to the terminology used to describe compassion fatigue. For instance, compassion fatigue is sometimes mistakenly referred to as "burnout," but more accurately, it describes burnout that has progressed to a higher level. Additionally, some researchers use

7   McHolm, Fran. (2006). "Rx for Compassion Fatigue" *Journal of Christian Nursing*. 23(4):12-19, Fall

the term "compassion stress" to identify the symptoms of compassion fatigue. Because the symptoms are not mutually exclusive, this book will use the term "compassion fatigue" to avoid confusion and redundancy. Note the similarities between the two definitions below:

**Compassion Stress-** A set of psychosocial and emotional factors caused by a specific event or series of events affecting helpers indirectly through another, such as a family member, friend, or client. Just one case or situation can have a lasting psychological effect. (McHolm 2006).

**Compassion Fatigue-** The "state of exhaustion and dysfunction (biologically, psychologically, and socially) as a result of prolonged exposure to compassion stress. We become exhausted by the exposure to experience after experience of emotionally draining clients who look to us for help." (Figley 1995). [8]

Both definitions accurately describe the emotional, physical, social, and spiritual exhaustion that overtakes a person and causes a pervasive decline in his or her desire, ability, and energy to feel and care for others. Such fatigue causes the sufferer to lose the ability to experience satisfaction or joy professionally or personally. Compassion fatigue is not pathological in the sense of mental illness, but is considered a natural behavioral and emotional response that results from helping or desiring to help another person suffering trauma or pain.

Some trauma experts hypothesize that people who choose helping professions have some form of predisposition to burnout that can later lead to compassion fatigue, due to strong tendencies toward self-identification with the helpless and disadvantaged, which can also lead to such clinical difficulties as projection, transference, and countertransference.

---

8  †† Figley CR. (1995). "Compassion fatigue as secondary traumatic stress disorder: An overview." In: *Compassion Fatigue: Coping with Secondary Traumatic Stress Disorder in Those Who Treat the Traumatized.* New York

This excerpt from the Journal of Christian Nursing, Fall 2006, describes how this level of compassion fatigue can affect those in the nursing profession.

> *Nursing care situations that contribute to CF-1 include a high turn-over of patients who are acutely ill, rotating shifts and changing job assignments. Those working in crisis-oriented venues such as emergency or trauma centers seem most vulnerable. As a result of CF-1, nurses become emotionally drained, experience stress-related illnesses and eventually leave the profession if the condition is not addressed. Whereas nurses with burnout adapt to their exhaustion by becoming less empathetic and more withdrawn, compassion-fatigued nurses continue to give themselves fully to their patients, finding it difficult to maintain a healthy balance of empathy and objectivity.* (McHolm 2006).

Like nurses, mental health professionals can experience similar reactions in that they tend to absorb a client's pain and suffering and relate on an interpersonal level where the professional boundaries become obscure. In helping professionals that deal with significant trauma, abuse on a much more emergent level requiring quick assessment skills, expedited treatment decisions, and an elevated level of response to sometimes life-threatening situations cause added stress and anxiety that can sometimes result in elevated anxiety and stress leading to clinical distress and the need for treatment.

People that are highly sensitive and attuned to the feelings of others tend to be drawn to the mental health professions. For this reason, the likelihood for compassion fatigue increases, as this sensitivity exposes greater vulnerability to take on a client's suffering and emotional distress. Demographics and personal history also have an effect on the degree to which a professional may experience compassion fatigue. For instance, a counselor with a prior history of traumatization may be more likely to experience compassion fatigue, as working with others who have been traumatized may bring up their own personal pain throughout the clinical process. Hearing vivid stories and graphic explanations of abuse can create relapse in symptoms for the clinician. In these cases, it is extremely important for the clinician to have an increased sense of self-awareness and to be alert to the signs and symptoms of compassion fatigue.

Mental health treatment and therapy require a level of empathy that surpasses most other forms of professional treatment. Therefore, skills are taught on all levels in order to provide effective treatment to our clients. Such skills as empathic and active listening, unconditional positive regard, and motivational enhancement techniques not only require a cognitive commitment, but an emotional one. All professionals are required to tune in to the emotions of their clients in order to provide feedback and redirection to maximize the therapeutic process.

However, these skills require close attention to the cognitive and emotional process for the therapist as well. In order for a mental health professional to be effective, it is imperative that they are equipped with a sense of self-awareness and insight with regard to their own feelings that may surface while providing treatment to others. Many schools of therapy and social work require therapy for students to assist in this process; however, many do not. Because the people drawn to this type of work are typically more sensitive to others, therapy is highly recommended to help the students and counselors continue to develop both personally and professionally.

## Vicarious Trauma

Traumatic stress reactions that result from critical or emergent clinical work are also sometimes referred to as "secondary" or "vicarious" trauma, and can be slightly different than compassion fatigue. Compassion fatigue tends to be more closely associated with this escalation of unaddressed burnout and emotional exhaustion. However, vicarious trauma reactions are the result of the helper being directly involved with a client or situation in a crisis, disaster, or other forms of acute traumatic events.

Symptoms of post-traumatic stress disorder experienced by the client can be internalized by the clinician, thereby leading to a form of PTSD known as secondary traumatic stress.

"The symptoms developed by persons suffering from PTSD, or secondary trauma, are nearly identical. The only difference is that with secondary trauma, the traumatizing event experienced by one person becomes a traumatizing event for the second person." (Perry, Conry, & Ravitz 1991)[9]. Until very recently, research has primarily focused on clients with PTSD; new research and practice implications are now recognizing that secondary trauma reactions are also a major issue for helping professionals as well.

While burnout and compassion fatigue may progressive, vicarious trauma is the emotional response to a single, acute, traumatic event. Research indicates that the more empathic a clinician is, the greater the risk of compassion fatigue and secondary trauma. Other risk factors include ineffective supervision, high caseloads with traumatized or emotionally complex clients, lack of workplace cohesiveness, and a lack of organizational and systemic resources.

As the need rises for specialized trauma-informed services, so does the need for effective self-care, supervision, and knowledge of vicarious trauma. As clinicians provide services to this highly sensitive population, they are hearing their clients re-live their experiences, sometimes in graphic detail of death, murder, abuse, destruction, and loss. The clinician needs to be protected from developing vicarious trauma (V- PTSD) in the effort

9   Perry BD, Conroy L & Ravitz A. (1991) Persisting psychophysiological effects of traumatic stress: The memory of "states." Violence update 1; 1-11

to maintain empathy. The symptoms of V-PTSD are similar, if not exactly the same, as if the clinician had been the victim of the trauma him or herself. V-PTSD is characterized by feelings of helplessness, fear, dreams or nightmares, elevated startle or panic response, anxiety, and depression.

It is imperative that adequate supports are in place to protect clients as well as clinicians. Regular and consistent supervision, one-on-one therapy, crisis intervention, personal time off, and other forms of therapeutic intervention should be readily available and accessible to clinicians who face a high risk of V-PTSD.

# Chapter Three:

# Who Is Affected by Burnout and Compassion Fatigue?

Compassion stress can affect anyone, in any profession. Stay-at-home parents who do not work outside of the home may also develop similar reactions due to the nature of their day-to-day routines and rising concerns about the present economy. The same may also be true for someone in the position of becoming a primary caregiver to an ailing parent or spouse. Compassion stress does not discriminate; rather, it can occur as easily in a tenured psychiatrist as it can in a first-year student of social work who finds him or herself overwhelmed. The truth of the matter is, wherever there is a situation where added demands for the care of others arise *in addition to* existing personal or professional responsibilities, compassion stress of some kind can result.

At the very core of undergraduate and graduate curricula in medical and mental health degree programs, the practice of empathy receives great emphasis. The majority of the focus remains in theoretical education, while practice issues focus on the client, and not the practitioner. Research papers, role-plays, and process recordings are used as tools of learning the art of providing unconditional acceptance to clients, with little or no emphasis placed upon successfully learning to disengage after a session, particularly when a client is in an acute emotional crisis. Medical and environmental causes of mental health and illness are studied at length; however, it is very rare that a course focuses on the emotional impact that these issues may have on the counselor. In fact, most counselors are almost socialized into the premise that because they are catalysts of positive changes for others, this also provides them with the effective tools to remain emotionally neutral and clinically objective in all cases. In essence, they learn to care for the needs of others before caring for their own, reinforcing the predisposition that the novice caregiver may already possess.

Additionally, schools pay little or no attention to the importance of self-care for clinical students. It would be ideal if new clinicians were taught about these concerns early on, and encouraged to make self-care a regular practice as they embark on a new career that demands time, attention, alertness, and high standards for empathy and compassion. Placing clinician self-care high on a list of educational priorities may help students and new clinicians avoid the possibility of burnout later in their careers.

However, the national work ethic itself places very strict demands and expectations on American workers. With the economy in a dubious state, workers are lending themselves to the idea that "more" is better in order to keep their jobs and their personal finances afloat. However, this notion of committing 110 percent to the workplace, taking work home, working weekends and overtime, and not taking vacations provides a false sense of job security and ultimately leads people to feel overworked and exhausted, leaving little time, if any, to engage in enjoyable or restful activities that are so important to physical and emotional well-being. Learning to manage stress and workloads, and finding a healthy balance of personal and professional activities can prevent a great deal of stress and anxiety.

The expectation that the counselor can easily engage and disengage with a client, even in busy clinical settings, gives rise to an increasing danger in the profession. A counselor who cannot provide empathy cannot effectively treat a client, and may perhaps create unintentional harm in the place of effective clinical treatment. Chronic stress reactions of helping professionals can also have a negative effect on the organization as a whole. For this reason, it is imperative that clinical professionals learn the proper tools of organization, self-care, and boundary setting in order to remain effective, while at the same time, promoting their own well-being, avoiding the inevitable emotional distress that can accompany compassion fatigue.

"Helping" professions at high risk for compassion fatigue:

- Mental health professionals–counselors, therapists, psychologists, psychiatrists
- Medical professionals–doctors, nurses, nursing assistants
- Emergency response personnel–police officers, firefighters, emergency medical staff
- Substance abuse clinicians
- Child welfare workers
- Crisis/suicide hotline or response staff
- Undergraduate and graduate students

The risk of burnout and compassion fatigue may be increased by the intensity and nature of the work involved. It's commonly associated with the everyday, routine hassles of working with others that has a significant impact on the clinical relationship, despite the fact that the cause may be organizational and not necessarily involve direct client contact. Time constraints, deadlines, documentation requirements, and lack of coordination with other team members or providers involved in client care can lead to emotional responses such as frustration and anger. Such situations in which caregivers feel powerless in meeting personal and professional expectations can lead to burnout, which can progress to compassion fatigue if unnoticed or untreated.

Below are statements made by clinicians regarding their clinical work:

*"Sometimes, I have so many clients booked in one day that I feel overwhelmed. I'm constantly looking at the clock, while trying to seem empathic. I hear so many problems in one day that the clients all seem to blend with one another, and before I know it, I'm giving back automatic responses, as if they had been prerecorded. I keep hoping that there is no crisis, or the client doesn't start crying, because I know that it will hold up my schedule and I'll fall behind for the rest of the day. I feel really guilty about feeling that way, and I don't feel that I am helping at all."*

*"There is so much drama at my agency that I just shut myself out. I go in, do my work, get paid, and that's it. I hear so much complaining from my clients, I don't need to hear it from my colleagues. We're all burnt out—I have to worry about myself."*

*"My agency expects us to be doing three jobs all at once, and still have the energy to be sympathetic to our clients. For every one client I see, there's about an hour and a half of paperwork that follows. I have such a huge caseload and I am drowning in paperwork. Clinical contact is the last thing on my mind."*

*"I'm having a hard time sleeping, because lately, I keep dreaming about my clients. It's like my whole life revolves around work. I dream that I am in session, or derailing a crisis, and I wake up exhausted. It's all I can do to drag myself into work in the morning, because it feels like I've been there all night."*

*"I was working with a young woman who had been raped during a burglary. She is explained what happened with such intimate detail, I started to shake during our session. Later on that night, her case was on the news and I had a panic attack. Now, I can't watch the news, because it will trigger my anxiety too much."*

# Chapter Four:

# Transference and Countertransference

Transference and countertransference in the clinical relationship also create a higher risk of empathic failure and compassion fatigue. Before learning the essentials of clinical self-care, it is vital to understand how and why transference and countertransference occur in a clinical relationship.

*Transference* and *countertransference* are terms originating in psychoanalytic theory, and have provided organizing principles in explaining certain developments within the "doctor-patient" relationship. (Sadock and Sadock 2003)[10]. These principles are the theoretical backbone of compassion fatigue, requiring complete understanding as part of the identification of a clinician's self-concept within the clinical relationship.

*Transference* is the process by which the client essentially transfers his or her feelings of a past or current relationship to the helper. These feelings can be positive or negative, conscious or subconscious. The nature of the transference is not constant, and can swing from one extreme to another. This transfer of feelings poses a large and powerful roadblock in the therapeutic process, and promotes a wide range of emotions within the client such as anger, fear, resentment, love, sexual attachment, or idealization of the counselor. More often than not, however, transference is mostly affiliated with the client's relationship

10 Sadock and Sadock (2003). *Synopsis of Psychiatry*. Philadelphia, PA: Lippincott Williams & Wilkins

with his or her parents, giving way to a virtual "re-creation" of these relationships if not quickly recognized and addressed.

Transference can occur with a client for many reasons, such as

- abuse or neglect as a child;
- parental/family substance abuse;
- parental/family mental illness;
- domestic violence/divorce;
- loss and grief issues; and
- addiction (client).

One effective method of recognizing transference in a client is continual assessment and observation. Does the client tend to idealize, make statements that are more personal than professional, or ask personal or intimate questions outside of the scope of treatment? Does the client threaten, lash out in anger, or appear suddenly withdrawn? Does the client often make statements that start with, "You remind me of..."? Does the client resist boundaries that maintain professional distance? If the clinician suspects transference, he or she is responsible for addressing it with the client and, in effect, renegotiating the clinical contract, if possible. If the client's resistance to the professional boundaries escalates, or if attempts to address and redirect the transference are unsuccessful, termination of the clinical relationship may be indicated.

*Countertransference* refers to the clinician's own sometimes-distorted view of the clinical relationship and is often the basis of subconscious expectations placed upon the client's behavior, or in some cases, preconceived notions regarding a client's motives for his or her behavior. As with transference, countertransference is usually attributed to the clinician's past or present relationships, causing emotions that vary in scope from extreme dislike to even eroticization of the client.

At times, the client's progress and compliance with treatment goals and expectations (or lack thereof) and can be a major contributor to countertransference in the clinician. A client who is not making progress as expected or who is especially resistant to treatment may invoke perceived feelings of inadequacy and failure in the clinician, creating tension or perhaps even hostility within the therapeutic relationship. This creates a reciprocal emotional reaction in the client, who likely in turn responds with negative behavior or "acting out," which will reinforce the countertransference in the clinician, thus creating an environment for ineffective treatment and the possibility of emotional harm to the client and/or the clinical professional.

Emotional reactions that the clinician can experience in countertransference:

- guilt
- shame
- fear
- anger
- resentment
- inadequacy/failure

A reaction of countertransference is not uncommon for clinical professionals; however, there seems to be a taboo around the subject in some clinical settings. This can occur for many reasons, but it would seem that the lack of disclosure to supervisors, colleagues, or even clients with regard to countertransference might stem from the clinician's fear of others perceiving him or her as weak, ineffective, or unskilled.

The reality is that a good clinician is able and willing to recognize his or her strengths as well as weaknesses, his or her emotional vulnerabilities, as well as areas of clinical expertise. All clinicians experience these situations, and need to avoid self-criticism that could lead to compassion fatigue. The ability to set appropriate limits based upon a solid sense of self-knowledge of the clinician is a good foundation for the development of a strong and effective therapeutic relationship, one that can either avoid or divert issues of transference and countertransference throughout the course of treatment. Developing these skills is a fluid process and should be an ongoing part of professional development.

For a clinician, the recognition of countertransference with a client can be a difficult process, particularly in situations where adequate supervision is not available. Often, the clinician's negative emotional reactions toward a patient will prevent him or her from disclosing and processing feelings. The clinician may worry that others will perceive him or her as inadequate, or the clinician may fear losing his or her job.

The following anonymous quotes illustrate some common examples of burnout, compassion stress, and fatigue:

"Sometimes, I get so burnt out with a client, that I have no tolerance or motivation to see anyone for the rest of the day. I don't have the strength or energy. I wish that I had someone who cared about my problems for once, instead of always fixing things for other people."

"I get very angry when a patient doesn't take my advice and goes to other sources—it feels like my credibility is in question. I'm a good clinician, and I feel like because I'm younger than most, my clients don't trust my clinical judgment. It's very frustrating!"

"I had a client that reminded me so much of my mother that I would literally cringe when she walked into my office. What was even worse was that she treated her children the same way that my mother treated me. I found myself constantly wanting this client to like me, even though she had burned many bridges with other professional helpers. When she became angry with me, I would feel the same feelings that I had as a child. Only when I finally sought supervision was I able to discover that I was seeking her acceptance and approval, and that my work with her was based on a countertransference reaction."

"When I tried to talk with my supervisor about a client that I was beginning to dislike, she immediately cut me off, saying 'That is your own issue, and you need to get past it quickly.' I felt very dismissed and ashamed, and never brought it up again. In the meantime, I started to resent the client and I felt trapped in my shame."

"I struggled with infertility for a long time, and was never able to have children. I had a client who was pregnant and using drugs. It made me so angry that she took her pregnancy so much for granted that she would behave that way, I just couldn't work with her."

To understand some of the emotional roadblocks that can occur between clinicians and clients leading to compassion fatigue, it is important to understand emotions; their origins; and how and when they can interfere with clinical care.

One of the most complex of these emotions is shame. It is important to differentiate this emotion from the emotion of guilt. Although many definitions seem to intertwine the two, shame and guilt are actually two very distinct emotions with their own accompanying beliefs and value systems. Both can be extremely powerful, and, if not recognized and dealt with properly, they have the potential to become definitive roles in the lives of both the clinician and the client.

This area of research has been largely avoided, but recently, there have been major developments in learning more about these emotions, which can either lead to or become the result of burnout and/or compassion fatigue.

*Guilt* is an emotion that usually describes the feelings experienced after an event or behavior with negative results or consequences, involving regret, remorse, and sometimes, resolve. It can be both constructive and a motivator for change, in that the person who experiences the emotion of guilt usually finds a way to correct the behavior, make amends, and learn to avoid the repetition in the future. It can also provide the springboard for rumination and self-pity, where the person experiencing this emotion can continue on a path that can lead to *shame*, if ignored or not resolved. It is holding up an action or behavior against our ethics, beliefs, and values, in order to find resolution. (Brown, 2007)[11]. Guilt is about *behavior.*

*Shame* is the key component to all unraveled connections, and has emotional, cognitive, and physical impacts. It is by far a more destructive emotion than guilt, and is rooted in negative self-identity that corrodes the self-concept. Shame is almost always at the core of empathic failure with clients. It does not drive constructive, corrective behavior; rather, it lends itself to other emotions such as feeling disconnected or invalidated, resulting in a tendency to attack or humiliate others as a defense against this powerful and painful emotion. Shame is accompanied by a low sense of self-esteem, self-worth, and a sense that this emotion is somehow deserved because of feeling devalued. Shame is not about behavior, but about *who you are.* (Brown, 2007).

Shame researcher Brene Brown writes, "In the mental health field, we recognize caregiving as one of the most stressful life events people face. When [women] talked about the anxiety, fear, stress and shame of being a caregiver, I could hear the demons of perfectionism in their stories. Regardless of the words spoken, I could hear them comparing the hard realities of their day-to-day responsibilities to their idealized images of stress-free, dutiful, and rewarding caregiving."

--------

11 Brown, Brene. (2007). I thought it was just me. New York, NY: Gotham.

# Chapter Five:

# Personalization and Perfectionism

When a helping professional begins to personalize a client's progress (or lack thereof), there is a high risk of compassion fatigue. As catalysts of change, counselors offer the tools and skills- based knowledge to his or her clients to help them learn how to help themselves. However, if a helper holds the view that he or she is also somehow personally responsible for those changes and for the success of those he or she helps, any lack of progress or treatment failure becomes an emotional failure to the helper as well.

Personalization is a form of cognitive error or distortion whereby a helping professional misinterprets or internalizes the therapeutic relationship, or the dynamics of that relationship, as a personal issue, achievement, or failure.

Often, a client's behavior can become personalized, and be interpreted as being directed at the clinician. For example, a cognitive behavioral therapist is feeling challenged by his client's severe symptoms of obsessive-compulsive disorder (also a form of personalization). He works diligently to research alternative ways of overcoming these symptoms, and develops a written "homework" task for the client to complete after a session, to be presented at their next meeting. At the next session, not only did the client forget the paperwork, but he also did not engage in the assigned task at all. The clinician becomes upset and personally offended by a perceived lack of respect for the extra time and effort in took him to develop this intervention, and he sanctions the client for not following through.

Feelings of professional responsibility can easily become feelings of personal responsibility, as helpers often base their personal identities on the work that they do. As rewarding as it can be to see a client benefit from professional help and interventions, it can also be equally as devastating when symptoms return or increase despite treatment. Helpers that begin to question their professional skills in response to treatment setbacks or failure eventually begin to question themselves as professional helpers, allowing for the possibility of thoughts and feelings such as professional or personal inadequacy.

Becoming too emotionally invested in any treatment case, without setting proper professional boundaries and adequate supervision, can create the perfect environment where compassion fatigue and vicarious traumatization can prevail. Using the client as the only gauge of successful intervention proves to be a high-risk practice, paving the way for transference, countertransference, and personalization of the treatment relationship.

In some ways, the professional relationship between a counselor and client can be extremely intimate, challenging, and at times, emotionally intense. As a client begins to share and disclose such issues as personal trauma, behavioral issues, or relationship problems, professional intimacy and trust should increase, which must be harnessed within the professional context without personalization of the changing dynamics of the therapeutic relationship.

Not all therapeutic exchanges are positive. For example, counselors who work with people with substance-abuse disorders, or those involved in the criminal justice system or protective services can encounter clients that are resistive, confrontational, and at times, even combative. In these cases, it becomes even more difficult for the helper to avoid personalization if the client demonstrates resistance to treatment disguised as a personal attack.

Helpers in hospice settings are also at high risk of personalization and internalization leading to compassion fatigue. Because hospice cases usually end with the client's death, the clinician can easily become fatigued due to a lack of positive interactions with the terminally ill client. The lack of improvement in a client's condition, and working instead with a steady decline in physical and emotional function can make it extremely difficult for the clinician to find any personal or professional satisfaction in his or her work.

Although a counselor can be effective in helping a client with such skills as increasing motivation for treatment and progress, this should not be misconstrued as a personal success within the context of a professional relationship. Conversely, as a client can learn to model the behavior, motivation, as well as emotional responses of his or her helping professional, the counselor can also find the opposite to be true. The clinician may find him or herself "feeding off" of the emotional expressions and dynamics of clients, an indication that professional supervision and boundaries are needed in order to preserve and maintain the working professional relationship.

Perfectionism, in psychology, is a belief that perfection can and should be attained. In its pathological form, perfectionism is a belief that work or output that is anything less than perfect is unacceptable. At such levels, this is considered an unhealthy belief, and psychologists typically refer to such individuals as *maladaptive perfectionists.*

Perfectionism has personal, professional, and sometimes economic implications. In our fast-paced society, we encourage the ability to perform multiple tasks with minimal effort and maximum efficiency. The clinical environment is such that these sorts of demands are placed on helping professionals from various sources—clients, third-party payment sources, community and government agencies, professional colleagues, administration, bureaucracy, and many other sources. As the managed care system continues to mandate service provision and standards, less emphasis is placed on clinical care issues and more is placed on process, accuracy in documentation, deadlines, and abbreviated periods allowed for treatment. Attempting to perform well both clinically and within the bureaucratic confines of the managed care system can create emotional strain on the clinician, who may often feel that clinical judgment and ethics are compromised, limiting the resources available for the delivery of the best possible plan for treatment for each individual client. This "do the best with what you have" approach to clinical care is disheartening and a challenge to personal and professional clinical standards.

The standards of expectation assigned to helping professionals—in *addition* to clinical work and expertise, such as paperwork, documentation, referrals, treatment plans, and billing—all make it very difficult for a clinician to effectively gauge his or her emotions, seek guidance, and take time to evaluate his or her own risk for compassion fatigue.

While encouraging our clients to embrace mistakes in judgment or errors in functioning as being a normal part of the human condition, the message is also incorrectly given that the counselor is in some position of authority and does not merit the same luxuries of forgiveness or learning through trial and error. The misperception here is that maintaining a professional demeanor dictates presenting the illusion of infallibility to our clients; eventually, the illusion becomes a behavioral response to the intense emotional demands that can sometimes surface in the therapeutic relationship. In essence, the behavior becomes a perception, inviting with it emotional responses that are incongruent to the clinical task at hand. Failure to maintain the façade of perfection can create feelings of clinical inadequacy and, eventually, become compassion fatigue.

# Chapter Six:

# Post-9/11 Compassion Fatigue and Secondary Trauma

Mental health clinicians often provide mental health treatment to those victims that have suffered psychological trauma after disastrous events. Research indicates that individuals working in the psychotherapeutic professions are among those likely to suffer adverse psychological consequences for direct client activities.

These situations affect the nation far outside the areas marked as "ground zero." The far-reaching effects can continue to devastate many aspects of American life, creating changes in the way the society lives from day to day. Because PTSD is not always an immediate response, many more people can be expected to manifest symptoms of PTSD in the years to follow. Many first responders who survive the initial event may later require care and attention because they experience illness, grief, disabilities, and loss. Now, more than ever, it is important that mental health professionals be professionally trained in dealing with such clinical issues, and equally prepared to self-evaluate their own psychological stability.

The aftermath of the terrorist attacks that occurred on 9/11/2001 bring forward new challenges. In a nation at war, concerns such as terrorism and military involvement have increased the need for clinicians with trauma-specific specializations.

Despite the increased need for specialized trauma treatment, the long-term effects of providing these services have received very little attention.

To date, there is little research on this topic. One study performed by Adams, Boscarino, and Figley in 2006[12] measured the effects of providing social services to the victims and survivors of the attack on the World Trade Center in New York City. The study was based on Charles Figley's concept that psychopathology associated with psychological trauma can be vicariously transmitted through the therapeutic process. (Sabin-Farrell &Turpin 2003).[13]

The professionals that were surveyed performed a variety of clinical duties following the attacks, such as direct rescue and recovery efforts, providing therapy to individuals that had experienced loss and devastation, or providing shelter and resources to families that had been displaced because of the attack.

The study used several variables requiring consideration in order to measure the level of compassion fatigue/secondary trauma in post-9/11 service providers. A clinician's level of involvement (first responders vs. workers helping after the attack) seemed to have a significant impact on the study's findings, as did the age and experience of the clinician, the level of supervision and agency support, and the psychosocial history of the clinician. The higher the level of involvement paired with a personal history of trauma seemed to correlate with a higher degree of vicarious trauma and compassion fatigue.

- The level of support available in the work environment
- The level of involvement with the disaster itself (first responder vs. post-crisis services)

12 Adams RE, Figley CR, Boscarino JA. (2004). Compassion Fatigue and Psychological Distress among Social Workers: A Validation Study of a Secondary Trauma Instrument. New York: The New York Academy of Medicine.

13 Sabin-Farrell &Turpin (2003). Vicarious traumatization: Implication for the mental health of health workers. Clinical Psychology Review.

- The psychosocial history of the clinician
- Years of education and experience of the treatment provider
- The existence and availability of a positive social support network

Although the researchers indicate there were limitations to their findings due to such factors as sample size and data collection methods, the results of the data appear to remain consistent.

The study offers several important preliminary findings. According to the findings, job burnout and compassion fatigue may not be unique to the mental health professions; nonprofessional caregivers may also suffer the same types of negative emotional and psychological impact in response to a community disaster such as the attacks on the World Trade Center.

Perhaps the most significant of the findings is that there seem to be clear and unique differences between burnout and compassion fatigue/vicarious trauma, supporting the idea that these two concepts are indeed separate entities. The initial findings strongly support the notion that compassion fatigue is "a unique feature of the workplace environment and is not merely a different conceptualization for negative life events, personal trauma, or lack of social support." (Jenkins& Baird, 2002).[14]

Unfortunately, there have been no clear and concise methods defined to distinguish the specific needs of the client and the mental health professional dealing with the aftermath of 9/11. Because the devastation of the 9/11 attacks continue to unfold even now, there are some limited state and federal programs designed to assist victims and their families. Statistics and studies are generally vague and unable to determine the number of people directly and indirectly affected by the attacks.

----

14 Jenkins SR, Baird S. (2002). Secondary traumatic stress and vicarious trauma: a validation study.

However, there is little support offered to mental health agencies and their employees that provide post-9/11 care, creating a higher vulnerability to job burnout and compassion fatigue. This is extremely significant to the mental health profession, not only for the United States, but worldwide, as further threats and incidents of terrorism continue to remain ominous

Clinical educators and supervisors require trauma-informed service training and continued education that is specific to caring for the victims of disaster; however, these resources are scarce and limited. Scholars and researchers have been unable to reach a consensus on which treatments are the most effective for the client, and, as a result, offer little advice to the clinician for self-care. As a result of the lack of information with regard to the clinical implications for victims and caregivers affected by disaster, recommendations for training and education are also vague.

There has been a great deal of discussion about how to effectively distinguish "expected" grief that may also appear such as survival guilt, suicidal thoughts/gestures, social anxiety, and specific phobias. However, because the DSM-IV-TR does not currently differentiate symptoms of PTSD related to terrorism from other trauma-related experiences such as physical and/or sexual abuse, it is difficult for a clinician to make the determination of PTSD based on the current diagnostic criteria. However, it is important to correctly recognize these symptoms as being specific to the trauma to recommend appropriate treatment methods. For instance, visualization methods or exposure therapy may be ineffective, more harmful, and because of the scope of the attacks, not possible. The clinician must take great care in planning for effective treatment while at the same time, avoiding the possibility of re-traumatizing the client.

Because of the lack of evidenced-based education and the vagueness of clinical treatment recommendations, mental health professionals charged with the task of treating disaster victims carry the additional psychological burden of being less than confident in treatment planning, and receive little support. This will invariably lead to an increased risk of job burn-out and compassion fatigue, as the prevention, protection, and treatment resources are scarce for the mental health professional providing post-crisis intervention work.

There is an increased need for highly trained and skilled professionals to help treat victims and their families who are suffering the effects of war, terrorism, and natural disasters. At the time of publication, the physical and emotional scars left by the terrorist attacks of 9/11 and Hurricane Katrina are still raw and require healing. The United States has seen numerous earthquakes, flooding, and a disastrous oil spill in the Gulf of Mexico. During these times of immediate crisis, now more than ever, mental health clinicians and emergency medical personnel are being asked to volunteer as "first responders" to the scenes of these tragic events. They are faced with witnessing painful deaths, disease, homelessness, emotional pain, and people who have experienced life-changing losses. They are charged with helping survivors deal with the emotional pain of grief and loss, helping to allocate resources, and regain some sort of balance in their lives.

Unfortunately, many of these "first responders" are a form of temporary assistance until some sort of stabilization is achieved. This has left many victims and their families—who are often homeless, jobless, and without medical insurance—without any services to help them get through any problems that occur past the initial crisis. Often these people suffer the lasting effects of depression, anxiety, and trauma-related disorders, which are progressive in nature without effective treatment. Clinicians often find themselves leaving these temporary assignments with feelings of guilt and inadequacy, and with the realization that the required work had only just really begun. Some may hope that their early intervention was enough to avoid long-term suffering and mental health issues. The need for skillful, specialized trauma-informed services on a national basis has reached an all-time high.

The same is true for soldiers and their families. There is great difficulty in returning from combat assignments to the world and life these brave men and women once knew, which can cause conflicts in their functioning in many areas, and especially with family members, who have been holding their breath waiting for the soldiers to return. After witnessing the horrific and devastating effects of war, being placed in life-threatening positions on a regular basis, witnessing (or sometimes causing) death, these soldiers are at high risk of anxiety-related disorders, major depression, PTSD, and substance abuse disorders. The need for clinicians with experience in treating military-specific trauma will continue to increase as continued deployments occur to areas that are seen as a threat to our national security.

Because there are no clear recommendations with regard to treating victims of disaster, it is important for clinicians to educate themselves as much as possible on the events and the possible psychological effects that the attacks had on those directly and indirectly involved. This can include:

- Understanding the roles performed by first responders; getting a sense of the types of support that was available to them during and after the crisis
- Evaluating past and current social supports
- Getting a clear picture of the individual's psychosocial history, including any past traumatic events that may have occurred
- Assessing prior and current coping skills
- Determining previous psychological treatment episodes and/or mental health diagnoses
- Becoming aware of medical factors that can impact treatment
- Understanding basic trauma-informed treatment methods and individualizing them to the victim's needs

It also important that while applying strategies for the treatment of victims of terrorism and natural disasters that the clinical professional maintain a strong sense of self-awareness of his or her own feelings and emotions with regard to the attacks and be able to avoid projection and countertransference while providing care.

# Chapter Seven:

# Early Identification Factors of Burnout and Compassion Fatigue

Anyone in a position to act as a caregiver or helping professional is at risk of burnout and compassion fatigue. The risks tend to increase with prolonged exposure to client-related traumatic events, crises, and/or vulnerability. Studies have shown that the greater the degree of compassion and empathy that a counselor is capable of providing to clients, the greater the risk of developing compassion fatigue. (Panos 2007).[15]

Warning signs and symptoms include the following:

- anger
- sadness
- grief
- anxiety
- depression
- headaches
- physical fatigue
- stomachaches
- constipation
- self-isolation/withdrawal from activities outside of work
- mood swings/irritability
- relationship problems with spouse and/or family

15 Panos, A (February, 2007). Promoting resiliency in trauma workers. Poster presented at the 9th World Congress on Stress, Trauma, and Coping, Baltimore, MD.

- avoidance of certain types of clients
- missed/cancelled appointments
- tardiness
- lack of motivation

As compassion fatigue progresses and evolves in severe forms of compassion fatigue, warning signs and symptoms include the following:

- insomnia
- elevated startle response
- hypervigilance
- flashbacks
- preoccupation with clients/families
- feeling trapped in the helper's role
- inability to separate personal from professional life
- feeling that money, rather than personal fulfillment, is the only motivation for work
- sense of worthlessness
- resentment toward work/clients

As the phases of compassion fatigue progress, emotional exhaustion presents itself, often in the form of stress-related physical illness, and often including (but not limited to) the following signs and symptoms:

- increased physical illness(es)
- increased fatigue
- physical exhaustion
- substance abuse
- depression
- anxiety
- extreme lack of motivation
- memory problems/confusion
- breakdown of normal functioning and coping skills
- irritability

At this stage of compassion fatigue, the helping professional is no longer able to cope and will be unable to perform professional tasks and caregiving duties without significant medical and/or mental health assistance.

Once emotional exhaustion occurs, it is imperative to seek the assistance of a professional, either a personal medical or mental health practitioner that specializes in trauma and stress-related issues, or, if available, an employee assistance program (EAP) offered by the employer. Unless the individual seeks treatment, work performance will continue to decrease, as will functioning in other areas, including personal, family, and perhaps financial matters. Emotional and physical health will continue to decline, which will only escalate symptoms into a level of severity that could require a more intensive form of outpatient or inpatient treatment.

# Chapter Eight:

# Avoiding Burnout and Compassion Fatigue

Although it is virtually impossible to avoid compassion stress altogether, the helping practitioner can use several precautions to prevent the stress of caregiving from escalating to higher levels of distress, such as burnout and compassion fatigue.

**Develop a good working relationship with supervisors and co-workers**: These types of relationships are very important in the helping professions and can serve as a mutual support system in times of crisis. Crisis workers typically work in fast-paced environments that require quick decision-making skills, often involving matters of life and death. It is important to be realistic about the work involved and the amount of time it requires to wind down or "debrief" from a crisis. Utilizing colleagues, supervisors, or mentorship is helpful in order to keep the anxiety level of the clinical responder at a healthy level.

Utilizing supervision time to express frustration, process emotional responses, and regain focus is a valuable tool in preventing burnout and compassion fatigue. Supervision can be somewhat of a therapeutic experience in itself, as during sessions, much of the clinician's emotional processes can be worked out by allowing the clinician to vent feelings and then gain the skills and insight to understand where those feelings originated.

Co-workers often find themselves consulting with their colleagues, which is also a helpful means of processing. Regardless, the client's privacy is paramount; it is important to maintain professional boundaries with co-workers at all times.

Boundaries that have become blurred by intimate personal relationships formed between co-workers can add to the stress and anxiety of the work environment, and can actually increase your risk for developing burnout. Recognizing the difference between professional consultation and gossip-related venting is very important. Negative breeds negative, and when processing or consultation cross the line over to negative complaining or commiserating, it affects the whole working environment. Although the development of a good working rapport with other professionals is highly recommended, it is best to stay away from forming bonds with co-workers that step over the professional boundary lines.

If possible, discuss or recommend ways that your workplace can help reduce stress as a whole. Activities designed for this purpose can not only increase support, but also provide a sense of professional community, especially in agencies that have a fast pace or deal with crises on a regular basis. It is important to meet either as a team or individually after a crisis to debrief, process events, and offer mutual support. Encouraging self-care in the workplace sends a clear message that not only is staff supported, but they are valued for their human and emotional experiences as well.

**Develop a personal plan for stress relief:** A personal plan to de-stress is can be a major factor in the alleviation of anxiety and other stress-related conditions. So many excellent opportunities exist to fulfill this need, many of which are low cost and highly beneficial. Whether scheduling yourself for a regular massage (some insurance companies actually cover therapeutic massage!), exercising, meditating, doing breathing exercises, practicing yoga, or just listening to music, it is important to take a few minutes out of your daily routine to take care of yourself and your emotional and physical needs. Several online resources are available such as support groups, videos, guided meditations, and Web sites that are dedicated providing support. If you have access through your wireless telephone company, there several applications available, such as courses or programs that you can take with you wherever you go. With all of these opportunities and a little bit of creativity on your part, it is easy to develop a successful personal stress prevention and relief plan.

Anxiety and stress tend to lie dormant in our systems until they manifest as physical symptoms, and by that time, it has reached a point where we need some form of intervention. Learning preventive strategies can actually change the thought processes that can lead to burnout and fatigue.

**Evaluate your lifestyle:** It's always a good idea to evaluate lifestyle and habits that could increase your risk for developing stress or a stress-related disorder. Busy lifestyles tend to dictate certain aspects of self-care such as eating habits, and sleep patterns. Poor diet and lack of sleep account for many stress-related problems, medical problems, irritability, headaches, reduced efficiency and productivity, and accidents in the workplace. Lack of sleep also can lead to increased caffeine consumption, which can lead to gastrointestinal problems with prolonged, heavy use. Many people drink several cups of coffee a day under the false impression that it will elevate alertness; however, excessive caffeine consumption actually leads to a crash of energy later in the day, which is counterproductive.

It's also a good idea to evaluate alcohol consumption, over-the-counter drug use, and similar lifestyle choices that can add to the risk of stress and other health-related concerns. The number of helping professionals that eventually require substance abuse-related treatment is growing at an alarming rate. This not only places your job at risk, but also poses a serious threat to your health and safety, and that of others around you. What starts out as a drink to "take the edge off" after a stressful day can eventually progress into dependence on this to cope with stress, depleting your natural methods of coping. It's a good idea to limit use of alcohol, especially when under stress, and use healthier alternatives to find relief from anxiety or fatigue.

It is also important to maintain your physical health by keeping up to date with your annual visits with your medical doctor. Failing to maintain your physical health can affect emotional and physical functioning, leading to larger or more severe problems later on.

**Counseling:** Although the Hippocratic Oath states, "First, do no harm," there is also another valuable saying in "Physician, heal thyself." Just as our clients need added support, so do counselors. Finding a therapist to help you help yourself, avoid stress escalation and help ease some of the burdens of professional and personal issues is an excellent way to manage stress and anxiety. This is particularly beneficial when needing to discuss professional or personal issues or concerns that you should not discuss at work. Having the added sense of support in both professional and personal matters with another professional that is neutral to both can provide you with meaningful opportunities for skills enhancement.

**Siesta:** If possible, utilize a ten-minute period daily to close your office door—or find a private spot at home—turn out the lights, and regroup. Organize your thoughts, do some deep breathing or stretching, and just take a break to slow down the pace a bit in the middle of the day. This not only will you bring you some peace during a stressful day, but will reset the pace for the rest of the day and provide you with some relief earlier, rather than later.

**Look around you!** What is your environment like? Are you working among clutter and stacks of paperwork, filing, and phone messages? This type of setting increases stress because as you begin a task, there are nagging reminders all around you of other things that you need to do as well. Take some time to organize your workspace. Ask for administrative help with filing needs, etc. If need be, return to your office after work hours so that you can clear up your environment without distraction. The sacrifice of a Saturday morning or a few hours in the evening can pale in comparison to the relief of organization and having a clear picture of what tasks are ahead of you. The same goes for your home environment. Ask for help in keeping things organized. Add pictures, posters, fragrances, music, and other aesthetic things to your environment that help you feel comfortable and relaxed. Not only will you feel more relaxed, hopefully, so will your clients.

**Know when to say when:** Our desire to be recognized as effective caregivers can sometimes overshadow our basic needs for self-care. It is so important that we are able to say no to an extra shift, or to an extra session, etc., when feeling overwhelmed in order to maintain self-balance. Being a team player and a reliable asset is always positive, but there are big differences between being a "team player" and overextending yourself. Eventually, you may find that you are building feelings of resentment toward others who don't make themselves as available as you do, or even toward your clients. Although, as helpers, we tend to look at ourselves as being able to fix problems for others, it is important not to martyr ourselves for our work. Learning how to say no is a necessary skill that should be used early on in order to avoid burnout. If, however, burnout has already occurred, saying no can also be a therapeutic tool, which, once put into practice, can be quite liberating, help free up time constraints, and offer emotional relief.

Setting boundaries with clients is also sometimes necessary when dealing with some clients who present as dependent on frequent contract. This is especially true for clients in agencies with walk-in clients as opposed to appointment-only clients. Clients with mental health and/or substance abuse disorders are also experiencing lifestyle changes as they recover, and part of the learning process is to set appropriate boundaries with some reasonable flexibility allowed. Not setting therapeutic boundaries can put added stress on the helping professional, which can lead to negative feelings, leading to compassion stress and fatigue.

**Ask for help:** One of the most important coping skills is knowing when you are feeling overwhelmed and asking for help to get things done. Learning to delegate, assign, or share work responsibilities is a valuable lesson in learning about your own strengths. Do not let pride get in the way of asking for help. When you become overwhelmed, your work performance suffers, client care suffers, and eventually, so do you. Asking for help is a skill that every helping professional would benefit from mastering.

**Humor:** It's true what they say about laughter being the "best medicine." Humor is also, when used wisely and appropriately, a great stress reliever. It can help keep things in perspective and remind us not to "sweat the small stuff." Having something that makes you laugh, such as a humorous picture or list of jokes (appropriate and not offensive when used at work) can be the perfect stress reducer.

**Music:** Another form of self-therapy is music. Listening to soothing music throughout your day can reduce stress and stress-related physical reactions, stabilize your mood, and provide a sense of comfort to both clinicians and patients/clients. Many stores and Web sites specialize in soothing, therapeutic music, which is now widely available to the general public.

**Creativity:** Being creative in your work can be uplifting and a way to manage routines that become dull or feel automatic. Within reason, and if qualified, try different ideas with clients such as music or art therapy, role-plays, games, etc. to enhance the therapeutic relationship and your motivation level.

**Utilize your benefit time:** Do not skip vacations, or be afraid of personal time. Avoid using days off to run errands or accomplish other tasks; it's a good idea to save this time for a road trip, a day home alone, or a day to just relax and enjoy. It is surprising how many people do not use their vacation or personal time at all. Denying yourself rest and relaxation is a mistake; many employers offer paid vacation time, so use it to your fullest advantage.

**Avoid office gossip and politics:** This dynamic exists in every work environment, and not only is it harmful and counter-productive, it removes focus, drains energy, and promotes a negative and sometimes hostile work environment.

**Exercise:** The benefits of physical exercise are endless. Exercise not only provides a healthier physical body, it promotes mental stability and well-being. It increases energy levels and is a highly effective stress reducer. Walking, aerobics, yoga, Pilates, and many other forms of physical activities help sharpen focus, build stamina, and enhance relaxation. The results of a regular exercise routine are almost immediate, and have long-term therapeutic benefits as well.

**Take a class:** If you are interested in something, learn more about it to increase your activity and satisfaction level away from the work environment. Many community colleges offer classes in art, music, dance, and many other recreationally based topics. Classes are inexpensive and require little time commitment.

**Journal/blog:** Writing is a highly effective form of therapy, whether it involves poetry, music, a journal, or a blog. Blogging can be an effective way to network and connect with other professionals that could lead to an increase in your peer support network.

**Turn off your phone!** We are all guilty of this. But unless you are on call, keep your work-related phone calls away from your home environment. This is also true of e-mails, faxes, or any other form of bringing your work home with you. Letting your professional life bleed into your personal life is counter-productive for you, your family, and friends. Setting limits and devoting 100 percent of your time to your personal life while away from work can actually help increase work satisfaction. Avoid calls from friends asking for "free" professional advice. Helping out friends is a positive thing, yes...but avoid allowing it to happen too often. Cherish your friendships as give-and-take relationships, and don't get sucked into viewing your relationships as extensions of your professional ties.

# Conclusion:

The unique, complicated, and sometimes, very stressful mental health profession can place practitioners at risk for burnout and compassion fatigue. As the field requires that professionals remain on the cutting edge of practice information, technology, and credentialing, added stress to maintain a positive and healthy outlook toward helping can add to the burden of an already-demanding profession. In addition to the emotionally taxing work with clients in crisis and emotional turmoil, dealing with requirements of the managed care industry, public, and organizational policy can create vulnerability that can lead to clinician burnout and compassion fatigue.

Today's economic environment, recent increases in terrorism threats, and dramatic natural disasters intensify the risk of burnout and compassion fatigue, creating an increased need for research and evidence-based practices for clinical self-care. However, much of the focus has emphasized treatment after the fact, and very little work gone into prevention and early recognition.

Because burnout and compassion fatigue can happen to anyone who provides direct client contact, no one is immune from developing symptoms. Doctors, nurses, social workers, firefighters, police officers, and emergency medical responders can all experience symptoms of fatigue and exhaustion that affect their professional performance and interpersonal relationships.

The most important approach for any caregiver is prevention. It is crucial that a clinician increase his or her emotional self-awareness and understanding of what burnout and compassion are and how to recognize the signs and symptoms early on.

Learning to identify cause-and-effect relationships, self-monitoring emotional responses, and asking for help are important tools in avoiding falling victim to the burnout trap.

Incorporating simple and cost-efficient methods to improve the physical and emotional environment can be highly effective in treating the symptoms of burnout and compassion fatigue. Taking care of basic physical and emotional needs can be a form of self-treatment so that he or she can lead a long, satisfying career while helping to develop and maintain personal happiness and well-being.

# Bibliography:

1. Figley, C.R. (1993b). Compassion Fatigue and Social Work Practice: "Distinguishing Burnout from Secondary Traumatic Stress." *Newsletter of the NASW Florida Chapter, June, 1-2.*

2. Thompson, Rosemary. (2003) "Compassion Fatigue: The Professional Liability for Caring Too Much": https://www.riskinstitute.org/peri/

3. Merriam-Webster Collegiate Dictionary (11th ed.). (2005). Springfield, MA: Merriam-Webster.

4. McHolm, Fran. (2006). Rx for Compassion Fatigue. *Journal of Christian Nursing.* 23(4):12-19, Fall.

5. Adams R.E., Figley C.R., Boscarino JA. (2004). *Compassion Fatigue and Psychological Distress among Social Workers: A Validation Study of a Secondary Trauma Instrument.* New York: The New York Academy of Medicine.

6. Figley C.R. (1995). Compassion fatigue as secondary traumatic stress disorder: An overview. In: *Compassion Fatigue: Coping with Secondary Traumatic Stress Disorder in Those Who Treat the Traumatized.* Ed. New York: Brunner-Routledge. 1-20.

7. Jenkins S.R., Baird S. (2002). Secondary traumatic stress and vicarious trauma: a validation study. *Journal of Traumatic Stress.* 15:423–432.

8. Sabin-Farrell R., Turpin G. (2003). Vicarious traumatization: Implication for the mental health of health workers. *Clinical Psychology Review*.23:449–480.

9. Salston M, Figley CR. (2003). Secondary traumatic stress: effects of working with survivors of criminal victimization. *Journal of Traumatic Stress*.16:167–174.

10. Figley CR. (2002).Treating Compassion Fatigue. New York: Brunner-Routledge11. Figley C.R. (2007). *The Art and Science of Caring for Others without Forgetting Self-Care, Gift from Within:* http://giftfromwithin.org/html/artscien.html

11. Pines, Aronson, and Kafry (1988).*Career burnout: Causes and cures*. New York: Free Press.

12. Perry, B.D., Conroy L. & Ravitz A. (1991) Persisting psychophysiological effects of traumatic stress: The memory of "states." *Violence* update 1; 1-11

13. Brown, Brene. (2007). *I thought it was just me*. New York, NY: Gotham.

14. Sadock and Sadock (2003). *Synopsis of Psychiatry*. Philadelphia, PA: Lippincott Williams & Wilkins

15. Panos, A (February, 2007). "Promoting resiliency in trauma workers". Poster presented at the 9th World Congress on Stress, Trauma, and Coping, Baltimore, MD.

16. Gentry, Eric (2002). Compassion Fatigue: A Crucible of Transformation. *The Journal of Trauma Practice* (The Haworth Maltreatment & Trauma Press, an Imprint of The Haworth Press, Inc.) Vol. 1, No. 3 / 4, 2002, pp 37-61.

Bibliography:

17. Weiss, L. (2004) Therapist's Guide to Self-Care. New York , NY : Brunner-Routledge

18. Boscarino, Joseph A., Figley, Charles (2004). Compassion fatigue following the September 11 terrorist attacks: a study of secondary trauma among New York City social workers. Division of Health and Science Policy, *The New York Academy of Medicine, New York, NY, USA.*

Internet Resources:

1. Traumatic Stress and Secondary Traumatic Stress— Hudnall Stamm  http://www.iusb.edu/~bhstamm/TS.htm

2. Professional Quality of Life Scales: http://www.isu.edu/~bhstamm/tests.htm

3. National Institute for Occupational Safety and Health— www.cdc.gov/niosh/stresswk.html\

4. Gift From Within—a non-profit organization serving PTSD clients and professionals. Web site: www.giftfrom-within.org

5. Eric Gentry: http://www.compassionunlimited.com/ © 2010 Compassion Fatigue Awareness Project. All rights reserved.

27994395R00036

Made in the USA
Lexington, KY
02 December 2013